The Milky Body

Mari Deweese

Nixes Mate Books
Allston, Massachusetts

Copyright © 2019 Mari Deweese

Book design by d'Entremont
Cover photograph from the collection of Lauren Leja

All rights reserved. This book or any portion thereof may not be reproduced or used in any manner whatsoever without the express written permission of the publisher except for the use of brief quotations in a book review or scholarly journal.

ISBN 978-1-949279-17-7

Nixes Mate Books
POBox 1179
Allston, MA 02134
nixesmate.pub/books

"Wenn du mich siehst, dann weine."
Děčín Hunger Rock

Contents

EISTAS

Aldonza … 1
Geld … 2
Surge … 3
Lightning Rod … 4
To a Crevice where the God Comes … 6
In Nero's Garden … 8
Leaven … 9
Today I laid down … 10
We don't exist apart from the page … 11
Avoid it like the Plague … 12
What Is, and Is Not Transmutable … 13

AUTUMNUS

Márgarét to Gerard, 20 years later … 16
Spit Play is a Foretaste … 17
O Caroler … 18
Nameless … 20
Black Sheep … 21
Draw … 22
Promise Me You'll Stain My Skin with Yours … 23
Freebleeder … 24
Ochre Dreams of Caerulean … 25
There Are No Painless Transactions Between Us … 26
Tayberries … 28
Alcyone … 29

HIEMS
- Delicia — 32
- Poem in December — 33
- The leaning grasses — 34
- Alone — 36
- Beneath the Ecliptic We Wait to Rise — 37
- Rustling — 38
- Tyto — 39
- Vice of Verse — 40
- Peekaboo — 45
- Fortune Favors — 46
- Mercurial — 47
- Do Not — 48

TEMPUS VERNUM
- Mae — 50
- Not to yield — 52
- How to Stop the Cold — 53
- A Song of Spring — 54
- A Remarkable Exposition of Bogus Scholarship — 55
- A Missing Anvil — 56
- Greenhouse — 58
- Rain Dancing — 61
- On and on and on! — 62
- Golden Shoes and Laughter — 64
- Atrament — 65

The Milky Body

Eistas

Aldonza

Surprises lurk
in all these doorways.
Which word
is the right name?
Logos, sweetness,
meridian, morte,
windmill, sloes –

will any of these release me?

A filthy rag symbolizes
a filthy rag,
and dirty water tastes like shit.

If my hate for you
were half as heavy
as all my hate for me
you'd never rise.

Geld

A pair suspended
over rooty
protuberance.

Sourcefingers clasp
limb, leaves from
joining. Mottled

fleshiness fills
in sunlight, swallows
it up in gulp

and inhale yellow,
filters, veins
bulge with a sweet

water. Pick us,
they
speak against

the sky. Snip
us. Take,
eat. This is my

Surge

What
ripples over
epidermal pillowdown
electric
erect or
languid as
the ocean as
the waves
collapse
crest trough
crest
billows
hemispheric and
transductive shiver
on
down vesselsides all
foamy
wet glistening.

Lightning Rod

Our clothes flung haphazard
across the cement floor
of the park pavilion
I lead you out
into the pouring night rain
waterslick bodies bare
and ready. We find
an open spot
in the middle of a mown
grassy knoll where the full
fury of the storm can be felt.
Nearby thunder not quite
as frightening
in the face of exultation,
I push my fingers into
the wetness of the grass and
root them into the ground
as you plant yourself
at the angle
of my acute body.
You stand tall
and erect and exposed,
both of us desperate

to feel that final
····jolt
shock
our spines.

To a Crevice where the God Comes

I will lead you, or you can lead me.
Either way, I go, armful
of earthenware, jarful of honey,
hand full of staccato as yours
grabs mine with wires
that cut
into my fingers, make me heavy with a certain bloody scent.
Today we pay
deep obeliskital
respect to what we worship.

Cracked film replays a yellow scene:
(s)Laughter.

A palm trails along the rock face.
Hyposensitivity demands
a rougher touch,
demands to feel everything.
Everything. Every demand is
To feel.

Revelry begins with an offering.
Pour the wine on me, let it soak in my hair,

make trails of purple stain down face, chest,
gathering at tips to drip into dirt,
brooks down back, lake between legs. Drink
me. Drink all of me.

The reel sputters, skips, comes back blue
sign hazy.

Was that him? Is he here?
          We must make more music.
A skin drum in my belly matches
the frenzy in your grazing. I need
to dance, now!
I rip you as a ripened
loaf offering asunder.

The walls seep. In darkness,
panic grips us.
The horned god comes.

All whir of machinery ceases. Fade
out. Fine.

In Nero's Garden

the most pure
incarnation of human
love is this: a swelling
bundle loosens and releases
fragrance from
calyx grip. What drifts
now on dusk zephyr coils
round walled within
eminence, blithely,
until it merges with
a newer scent: those of faith
ornamental, bright lanterns
offering all of light
a skewered body gives.
These heady shapes
flicker as they are
thrown against the walls and
the silhouette is love.

Leaven

It's the heat inside,
hugs all these lives
worked deep into
my dough, humidified,
that gives me lift,
makes me
rise.

Today I laid down

in the middle of
the street. I let the tread
tear me as the weight
of metal bodies crushed
my bones, and I
kept thinking,
(with pieces of my brain
smeared like oil on
the asphalt) that the

                    stars

we don't see in the day
from our respective
hemispheres, still hold
beauty, even if some

aren't alive anymore.

We don't exist apart from the page

She drags the soft tips of her fingers along his collar bone, both moving inward slowly, just barely meeting over his sternum before returning outward to trace the side of his neck.
Lifting her eyes from the movement, she plants a level gaze at his.
"Promise me one thing," she says, bending both pointers sharply, the edge of nails slicing into skin.
"If it's gonna be sweet…" Fingers meet once more in the middle, the trailing lines of raw pink connect. She sinks in deep and rips downward as she whispers, "…don't write about it."

Avoid it like the Plague

Not enough attention is paid
to the cliché anymore. The poor sod
is immediately written off as if
he offered nothing but an awkward
limpdick pic after an hour or so
of introductions and do-you-like-?'s,

written off as if to be a cliché is
to be expected, and apparently
nobody wants that these days,
we all demand the NEW! Make us
FEEL, we scream, because
talking in an inside voice about
what's really real is also cliché,
but we're not hipsters – HOW
FUCKING DARE YOU?! – cuz
that's also, also cliché, and all of

it echoes back
as we scream from a well
with no water, 'FEEL!'
Feel, feel. 'DARE YOU!'
dare you, air you.
Cliché, liché,
-ché.

What Is, and Is Not Transmutable

If I ever loved him
it was gold, bright Zöe
running into the hands of death.
If I ever loved him
it was soft, water without
substance, an utterly useless issue.
If I ever loved him
it was warm, the ripened bloat-
meal of cadaverous gas in the sun.

I
did.
Didn't
I

become
a graven image
of a perfect god,
my insides slippery,
waiting for water,
waiting for intrusive
fire, waiting for some
passing beak to poke

and rip open a
                release from my
residual dyings, concealed
inside my gold
my soft
my warm,
        my love.

The waiting is not worth it.
There will never be enough
enchantment in this myth
to crack my eyeballs open,
extract, melt down the jelly,
and revivify the rose
that is only smoke,
and only stone.

Autumnus

Márgarét to Gerard, 20 years later

Lead flesh
falls from
false lips
lays on floors

of dead thresh
yellow leaves
felt flame

red under
the willow.

Spit Play is a Foretaste

Or a prequel to
the grave.
Open wide, my love.
Wider still, (yeh fookin slut)
wider, wider, while
the white ball grows
with every transference.
Pale strings spill,
froth out
and run down,

into the most endless of mouths:

O Caroler

Viewed through waves,
 a great height
 of years
 appears to gape
a   g   u   l   f
from   here
      to   there.

And should you look
out your backdoor
                        tonight
        and see
a light on the water, the
milky body
half
submerged
                in ink
is mine,
a failed beacon, siren

transmogrified
      into
            narcissus, a

delicious
low
serenade rolling me
under,
as I keep   on   singing, not

waiting for
my hand to   loosen
        the   knots,
            knowing I never will loosen,   knowing I do

not sing
       for you
but I
will never cease.

Nameless

A hagfish eats by latching
gaping hole of razors
to the anus of a victim.
Sucks out all the tasty treats.
Disengages, lets the hollow
carcass with the shocked
expression sink to be
another meal or thirty.

Needles in my cervix.
Strangers staring up my ass.
Talk to me about French Presses.
I'll tell you how jasmine pearls steep
to make syrup-tea that tastes like
the smell of honeysuckles.
Flip that switch. (How odd, to have
one's insides vacuumed out, be told
I am still alive.)

Black Sheep

When my love began to rot,
and her sweetness lingered everywhere
like plums, black skin split
to let a swarm of flies feast on liquid
yellow flesh bulged out,
I began to feed her
bamboo stuffing.
I pulled the long white filaments
apart, so like the soft cloud
love she still Possessed,
weblike, watching It
float through my fingers. Then piece
by piece I pushed them down
into her mouth, cracked open,
and with my loss, I felt her,
filled her, by strange Taxidermy,
with my three bags full.

Draw

Face to our own
faces, weapons at

the ready—
    (blank)
  gun itching, bow
notched—the sketch

of our life colors the winds,
        big
  belliedcanvasblown
      wide.
     From
    out of lips
comes the breath
from out of our veins, the blood,
the beat
      from out of the   universal
deck   our irrespective hands:
steep
signed salary

to be paid   in full
to the keeper
      of the tolls.

Promise Me You'll Stain My Skin with Yours

More words in more tongues
exist in the mouth of relativity
than all the tongues that ever
uttered them.
They span outward
like Hopkins' shook
foil, flaming, brightening,
destroying.
When will we learn
the only lesson of permanence,
the importance of ephemeral?

And these words –
these scratchings on the surface –
and *these* words –
these effusive vibrations –
vanish from memory
as they never do from fabric
galactic: they are
the dark matter

the only matter.

Freebleeder

I used to think that
bleached and processed
tree pulp would
be enough to catch and carry
emptied contents
of my womb.
But I am older now,
accessing and liberating
the wiser pain.
I let flow a funnel
into the world, knowing
what I did not know,
that words, like blood,
don't belong in a can,
and only cling to inside walls
for so long before
the source goes septic.

Ochre Dreams of Caerulean

The same sadness
that feels like home
        inhabits:
the resonance of the percussive rain;
the tingles in my scalp and down my
spine
from fingertips tracing
the path I weep across
        hollow eyes,
across sensitive skin on the tip
of my nose; the silence that is
less quiet
than an ocean of blood inside
my ears as I watch the woods
        exhale,
let go, the madder deep descending as
we do, becoming through breakdown:
O horizon,
awaiting
illuviation.

There Are No Painless Transactions Between Us

I suppose –
if the Muse is me –
then summoning
her specter
on the spot is nothing.
Constant companion,
when companionship is wasted,
when the silence is not needed,
when the shadows on the inside
of my brain look too much
like nothing, if you are
the Muse, then come forth –
I call thee! – and speak
through these
unoracle lips. I
suppose, there really is only
the shadows
and silence – after all,
the Muse is dead, because
the Muse is death, and all
the scribblings,
half-mad mutterings,
clawings through the mud

of memory are only
the echoes of a scream
that died on the airwaves
a very long time ago.
Ten or ten thousand, the ticks
mean she is paid
and dearly for the service
she renders in any capacity
to this poet.

Tayberries

on her lips are bloody
fingerprints

from all the victims
as they tried

to claw their way out
of her mouth.

Alcyone

Seven points on a chart.
Widdershins we go, round and round,
scuddy in ripped 'nets, dragging
the bottom for loot and lost bodies.
Seven throats on a block.

Scythe in air, the horned one screams
and all is dark and covered in the heat
of rut. Iron in the streams make
red prayers from open graves,
fresh dirt unearthed for later glories
(l'orgies) to be had upon soft mounds.
A middle aged fire burns blue.

Seven winds from the corners.
Fold up the maps and list to one side,
hear slaps of deep beasts beating,
flutters in a pit but Maia awakens
with a spurt of moonmilkiness,
blessed by all three of the hunter's
belt licks across backside of her sky.
Seven sisters on a pinhead.

Each sucks a different substance out
from the web as it floats: crystal,
opal, corn kernel, and conch,
bloodstone, propolis, and salt, each
swallowed with great gulpings and
followed with moans of satedness.

Seven stars from a crown.
Festivities for ecstatic first busting
bring our sun into folds of wet
while we sing brightly of wounds
on sacred heads hung from twine.
Seven thorns on a vine.

A belly opens and we pour
the sand of a year into it
knowing that when the hero sinks,
his face will forthtell the direction
 of the imminent(or)cosmical setting,
second or seventh coming inside this
cloudoven crawling up a tortoise spine.

Seven points on a pale hart,
on the hardwooded rim of the west.
And the braying of bitches after it.

Hiems

Delicia

If she presses her mouth to your ear,
lips open nebulas, and lets her tongue
slither, INTO your ear, past membrane,
past tiny banging bones, past nautilus
guard, to lick the edges of your brain,
gently
at first, then harder, encircling the whole
damn thing with her amazing muscle, then
squeezing, pythonic, until what matters
collapses lung-like in splattered waste,
you would believe then when she tells you,
mouth pressed against your ear,
'I am the real synonym of the word
for the place where dead men come
to kill anything left alive inside them.'

Poem in December

It was, he said,
His thirtieth year to Heaven.
I've wondered a hundred
Times if Heaven was meant
As optimism, or if a more
Euphemistic irony underlies
The reference paradisic. What
I mean to say is, was he skipping
All a-droll up those slopes
expecting to ascend towards
Some eventual pinnacle?
Because I know only the one hill,
and I've been thirty years falling
headlong down it, but I still
have not reached the bottom.

The leaning grasses

In the empty spaces
in the between of notes
hanging from staff lines
trailing from the sky

In between what falls
what drops crystallized
fractal in five/eight time

cold lingers a coda

A distance between
the spread of degrees
tetrahedron a caesura

echoes of a glowing

measure in the hush
half step in silence

almost covalencies
amid the swirling
in empty spaces
in distances between

I swear I can hear us
aching for music

Alone

There isn't enough tea
in my kitchen
to drown the awful weight
of being alone
(in my kitchen)
with only one cup's worth left.

Beneath the Ecliptic We Wait to Rise

Last year's nest and all that.
Shell pieces scattered, pin-stick
hurtful with that pigment left
only in fragments. Hatching
is one way to freedom
and an egg cannot
release without first
cracking.

Twigs, and twine,
hair, and wire
make home.

An absence
of heat equals death. Embryonic
suspense – floating
yolky in limbo – waiting
in palm for a sign to move on,
for the throwing of
a cold kill
switch..

Rustling

The rustling grows insistent.
Is it that thing
with feathers hiding? Or
that curse left in the box?
Can you catch it?

All tangled up tight bound
by the gore of birth, split
rib cage jagged, still meaty
and laid upon the ground as if
it were the good, acceptable,
and pleasing offering
to exchange for what
the holly holds.

Tyto

If she, being sage, intuits a loop through which
 the eye is seen as seer,
forgive her only in the instance that she asks
 for asking or, if sight
demands more mercury than silver, grant her
 mercy when she speaks
in raventongue with wild in six eyes snowy.

Vice of Verse

1.

Voices.
No one listened, no
one listens. Can we
still hear them when
trachealis muscle
rots, leaving
only cartilage ring
and partial rings
(if left intact and not
incinerated or
obliviated by COD)
through which only
imaginary air would blow
ghostly?

Are they echoes that
exist as imprints in the
atmosphere? I hear that
matter, energy is only ever
transferred, but if it
was never recognized

as mattering before will
the void recognize it after
all? Would any of us
recognize, remember,
something that we did
not know, never noticed,
never acknowledged
as needing to be seen
or known? Are the faint
brushes of noise we can't
place, in spite of our
strained ears, echoes
of ourselves from time
future, from whence our
breathlessness begs
anyone to prickle hair
on neck, in ears, in this
time, present, as no other
time exists?

II.

In the desert where we rode
for days and days and all
our life turned into dust
with every step and scurry

of whatever creature,
whatever falling rock,
we waited, and our sides
grew numb with the waiting,
and our eyes began to boil.
And as they down our dirty cheeks
began to drip, we opened our mouths
wide and swallowed the regurgitated
gift from our mother.

And in this time, that's neither
a beginning or a middle or an end,
the paths that cross become the oaths
we choose and choose again or
the ones we dismiss and lose.
And in this time, that's neither light
or dusk or dark, should paths cross
in a muddle or tangle perhaps
unraveling the red yarn will lead us
to the footsteps we made but had
forgotten in our wanderings.

We climb as marsupial
children into the pouch
of tenderness wherever

we may find it – we do not
know any other way
although we may not
know we knew it.
And though we fry
under this lamp
we nestle deeper
into the womb
feeding our voice
through umbilical waves
as though it matters.

III.

Avoid interrogation.
Avoid extrapolation.
Avoid asphyxiation.

IV.

And if you made a mark
carved into a beech, yew,
or ash, soft wood white
and waiting to take the tip
of the blade of genius,
then perhaps the path you

chose, though it leads
to a bluff (and heights make
you dizzy) will still carry
you into the grave knowing
you were known by one.

Does cartilage rot? Or does
it rust? The throat knows,
the voices know, and I must
try to listen for an answer.

Peekaboo

In the shadows,
behind a tree or
under a bed,
my heart full of
adrenaline makes
hiding a certain
sort of high.

And now, playing
but not playing
that same game grown
up into landscapes
of permafrost and always
dark, I peek
sliverface around to see
if what seeks me
sees me, or if
I am still
safe, the loud
sound of my heart
bursting my ears
with blood.

Fortune Favors

I have always heard
that those who find
four-leaf clovers are
the lucky ones.

But I know the real secret now:
you spend enough time staring
at the ground, at the sameness,
and any different
Thing
any sign
of change will always
leap out like a lizard
tongue into the corneal field.

The fact that we feel
fortunate to find
a mutant piece of plant matter
should scream to all
that
      lucky
is not what we are.

Mercurial

We do not eat ourselves.
We do eat. Ourselves.
We do not writhe in vain.
We do writhe. In pain.
He says spiral,
She says helix,
twisted words wind up a
flick, loop loosely like a wrist
downshaft.
White. What is white?
What questions can you ask it?
What image do you see?
She – mirrormorphological
atypical solid, solis, solace, slake
and silver, quickened to
protean blackness of these serpentine
intentions equals synthesis.
Conjugation may be met,
may yet be eaten under
wings: we are the burning ones.
We are the burning.
One.

Do Not

resuscitate what has been
buried since the second
death of self. frostbitten
tree of life says your mouth
is the grave, but mine,
mine is your grave.

Tempus Vernum

Mae

She is magenta.
and when slant
of sun
sideways through
iris slides, purest red
burns a febrile
beam straight
through a keyhole
in the partition.
A sigh, an apparition
shuts itself within
her folding,
and there is only
everblue,
stretching
into the second heaven
collecting dust diffusions
for a memory.
Cast
in moonlight she
fluctuates: becomes
under whole orb pair
of ovulating lips.

and when the sickle is
a gash
in blackness, she is wine
spilling
the secret to reading
treeleaves
down the jaw
of shadows.

Not to yield

As much as I can
I cannot.
As much as I have
I haven't.
My sovereignty
a remade
maidenhead – my will
will intact remain.
This is my inch.
A grey day is love –
wind that numbs
white fingers helps
me grip a harder pen
and sharpened nib
more whittled wets
the paper better, bleeds
a clearer wound.
What waves may take
me under, come.

How to Stop the Cold

Go outside at 4:ish in the morning.
Wear only boxers. Breathe in icicles.
When one tears open your trachea
Whistle from the wound a cardinal
Tune. Curl and flex fingers. This will
Keep knuckles blooded, Or The skin
will crack and clouds Will burn you.
Cough a hefty wad Of cardiac tissue
Out on the ground and smear it with
Your big toe to write a name Where
you stand. Close your eyes. listen for
equilibrium coming From the forest
between your ears. Set the saplings
on fire when you breathe out flames.

A Song of Spring

Flinch –
and the battle is flung far
too deep in these
trenches. What
wrenches hands from triggers, pulls
pins from fingers, finds
cross-hairs only fixing on air or other
unmarkable targets is this:
twitching limbs, spasmodic
and blooming vermilion, blood-brain
switching to accommodate pain which
sings with the wail of dropping
shells. Find my body, or what is left.
They say love is a war
and my gore feeds worms, wolves,
birds; in the cleft of my jaw
rests a nest made of hair
and three blue eggs lie waiting
to break.

A Remarkable Exposition of Bogus Scholarship

Eliot, in his alleyway chat
with Dante, was so certain
of his own irrelevance,
of all poets'
irrelevance.
Future words will be
written, and older words
will be rendered
obsolete
as unseen
concrete.
With all his sensitivity, I wonder
if he would take offense
to my plotting,
far-reaching desire
(How he avoided that word!)
to get his own
words permanently etched into
the thinnest of skin.

A Missing Anvil

If I listened harder,
I might could hear the clanging
that echoes like a nightmare
on the inside of his skull,
the sound of all the wails
of what is left of youth, carried into
the black hell of greedy mouths
with no song to serenade
the descent into the belly.
Flames leap up against
the walls inside the eyes
that see so much, but turn
to granite when the light turns
and the world goes yellow.
A great burning grows.
And should I add such tinder
as I have with others who have
more, or less- the bundle
does not matter, only
the desire to burn- when the sun
is even and night is even
for once in time,
to feel the heat of those

voices biting over bodies
of earth, mounds that ache,
to dance in the shadow
of a sehnsucht for home?
Bring the buckets.
There is still much blood
to be spilled before
the serpent eats itself
into a future for this
hammer to strike.

Greenhouse

You're either born
an old soul – or
you ain't. After
seeing through
a thousand eyes,
everyone's
a taint.
But, oh! To be
new, fresh eyes
blue, and wholly
unashamed
to see
how change
is still a thing
to do.

Goddamn punks,
he said.
Goddamn kids.
He saw the bareback
imprint in the moist
earth, the indentations
on either side

so obviously belonging
to a weight-bearing
pair of knees, the smears
on the inside glass,
the knocked-over pots,
inhaled the lingering
staleness of an after-act
cigarette, and other,
darker scents, and he
was so wholly wrong,
because neither of us
are kids anymore,
we creep vine-like
towards middle age
surely, swiftly, and grow
much slower now
than when we were still
young, and bright,
before we were wasted,
so many times nearly
compost, before so many
lifetimes had passed
through our fingers,

before we even met.
But then again,
maybe he wasn't,
maybe that crotchety
old ass was right, and who
snuck into his greenhouse
that night, and grew fast,
and strong, were two
things tired of surface
roots, sunless living,
that decided to sprout
new leaves and turn
our blooming faces
to the light once
again, like children,
innocent,
breathless and
gasping for breath,
gasping
gasping
at the glass
that housed
us.

Rain Dancing

I hear them whispering over there
as though they know some secret.
They pen
tenderness with their leaky nibs,
and write out desire, wet grip on
the stem.
You could buy all of their words
with your breath if you wanted.
And then
we could laugh in dark thunder,
throwing all their pages up, and
with them,
every last whisper, every secret of
tenderness, of thunder, knowing
that when
the looseleaf falls into puddles like
petals around us, the thin blue ink
will swim.

On and on and on!
(A shameless theft from James Joyce)

Amidst dream
I saw the slate
of curved thighs
and felt
the slither of a strand
of seaweed
up the back
of mine.
We locked eyes,
myself and I,
my heaving feathered
breast gone grey
against the current.
In this exhilaration
let me live
always, always to create
to swirl dark waters
with my foot,
such beauty
as I may have lost
to rise as what
once was plumbs

the salty plumage
of our mind.
And I, crane-legged
and flushed,
will wake and cry
and live again, and again,
and again, crashing
as a wave must
crash onto the stones
of this vocation.

Golden Shoes and Laughter

Clear economy.
Syntax, diction, metaphor:
Syllabic surgery.

Atrament

I.

The sacred wounds above me bleed
and I, pierced by both
fire and flame, melt as skin
liquifies and bone splinters,
cracking marrow running black
down the sticks of kindling
that my body used to be.

II.

Isabelline: the daughter
of skin and stretching, bleached
by the sun, dried to hardness,
rolled and warped to be pliable.

I love you.

I am nothing
– a waste
leaking
into obscurity –
without you.

III.

A million pounds per square inch implodes
aluminum-can creatures all around in the dark.
Softly tentacles sweep over the faces of
phosphorescent deep ones gliding through
the cold to keep the sac of wonder flowing
and safe. Within the secret place amongst
the horror of suffocation, magmatic
risings call and surge brilliant oozings

IV.

From a branch bulging,
I am picked prematurely with intent,
vibrant green and not yet hard.
Stabbed with a fork to penetrate
the flesh, soaked in brine
with cloves, molasses, peppercorn
for ten days until the death
and
resurrection is complete.
Sliced for intense and smokey
flavor, on toast and other tidbits.

V.

Breathe, o people.
Pull into your selfs
the magic of what
I am and how I do
what no other has
though ages have
passed as fluidly
as I do from well
to well to well to
well because all
minds are a well
and what flows
from one nib
or another is
spread in an
atramentous
love song
for you all
and not a
stroke or
dip has
been a
waste.

Acknowledgments

Certain poems have been featured in *Setu Mag, Western Voices Edition; LiveNudePoems; Three Drops in a Cauldron*, and on *Crude Language*, the album by bloodlikewine

About the Author

(Mari) Deweese hangs out in dark bars with loose morals and plays musical poetry with her band bloodlikewine, a collaborative project. In between the gin, the green smoke, and the mean reds, she manages to hoard pages of specifically crafted poems that sometimes end up in something as organized as a manuscript. Her first book, *Kinky Keeps the House Clean* was published by Nixes Mate in 2017. *The Milky Body* is her second work, to be followed by *Series from (behind) the Vale*, also from Nixes Mate.

42° 19' 47.9" N   70° 56' 43.9" W

Nixes Mate is a navigational hazard in Boston Harbor used during the colonial period to gibbet and hang pirates and mutineers.

Nixes Mate Books features small-batch artisanal literature, created by writers who use all 26 letters of the alphabet and then some, honing their craft the time-honored way: one line at a time.

nixesmate.pub/books